Without A Backward Glance:

New and Selected Poems

By The Same Author

Fiction
The Sound of My Voice (novel)
Night Visits (novel)
The Tilting Room (short stories)
Vivaldi and the Number 3 (short stories)
Coming on Strong (novella)

Poetry
The Wonnerfu Warld o John Milton
Stretto
Creatures Tamed by Cruelty
The Exquisite Instrument
Ragtime in Unfamiliar Bars
Histories of Desire

Drama
The Music Box
We've Been Had
Blending In

Opera Libretti
Markheim
Dark Kingdom
Faraway Pictures
Good Angel, Bad Angel

RON BUTLIN

Without A Backward Glance:

New and Selected Poems

To Ida,

with my best wishes,

Ron Butlin

b arzan

BARZAN PUBLISHING

13ᵗʰ October '07

Published by Barzan Publishing 2005

Barzan Publishing Limited
Windrush Millennium Centre
Alexandra Road
Manchester M16 7WD

www.barzanpress.com
info@barzanpress.com

First published in Great Britain in 2005 by Barzan Publishing

ISBN: 0-9549701-2-8

CIP Data: A catalogue record for this book is available from the British Library

Designed by Artista-Design

Printed and bound in Jounieh, Lebanon

This collection is for my friends and fellow poets
over the years, for my musician friends, my golf friends
and, of course, for Regi. Also for Neil Oughton,
who made it happen!

Foreword

'This very fine collection contains work selected from previous volumes plus a substantial batch of new poems. Butlin's poetry has evolved a subtle interplay between fact and fiction, with tones and moods heavy with desire, or light with enjoyment, sweeping up the occasional swathe of history but always returning to the acutely expressed personal and immediate.

Among the new poems here, there are reflections on Scotland in an untried phase of its history, moving stories of human loss and change and love and desperation, pungent recreations of Schoenberg and John Cage, and an evocation of the very different music imagined by a boy 'in the absence of an orchestra in his muddy Scottish village'.

The writing is precise and thoughtful, the book will give much pleasure.'

Edwin Morgan

Acknowledgements

Grateful acknowledgement is due to the editors of the following newspapers, magazines and anthologies where the poems first appeared: *Times Literary Supplement, New Statesman, Poetry Review, Ambit, Poetry Scotland, Edinburgh Review, Poetry Ireland, The Scotsman, Sunday Herald, The Herald, Aquarius, Bananas, Brunton's Miscellany, Chapman, Lines Review, AMF, The Antigonish Review, The Dark Horse, Descant* (Toronto), *Encounter, The Green River Review, Lot 49, Akros, Quarto, The Scottish Review, Words, The Sou'wester, Southfields, The Big Issue in Scotland, National Book League Writers in Brief, New Edinburgh Review, Paris / Atlantic, Verse, The Red Wheelbarrow, The Poetry of Motion* (Mainstream), *Scottish Literature in the Twentieth Century* (Scottish Cultural Press), *The Best of Scottish Poetry* (Chambers), *The Faber Book of Twentieth Century Scottish Poetry* (Faber and Faber), *Scottish Poems* (Macmillan), *Scotlands: Poets and the Nation* (Carcanet / SPL), *New Writing* (Vintage / British Council), *Such Strange Joy* (Shore Poets / inyx), *With Both Feet off the Ground* (Dumfries and Galloway Libraries), *Under Cover* (Mainstream Publishing), *Poetry Book Society Christmas Supplement, The Web Poetry Project of the Poetry Library at the South Bank Centre, Forward Book of Poetry* (Forward Publishing), *Carapace* (Cape Town, South Africa), *Unknown Is Best* (Mariscat Press), *Variations on a New Song* (Scottish Poetry Library), *Nova Scotia* (Mercat Press), *Present Poets* (Royal Museum of Scotland), *Goldfish Suppers* (The City of Edinburgh Council).

Some of the poems were first published in a bilingual edition of the author's work: *Nuestra Porción de Buena Suerte* (Hiperión, Madrid, 2002), in *Six Poètes Ecossais* (Editions Telo Martius, Côte d'Azur), *La Traductière* (Paris), *orte* (Switzerland), *Literatura Ukrania* (Ukraine), *Dienovidzio* (Lithuania), and in *Familia: Revistá de Culturá* (Oradea, Romania, 2000).

The Voice Inside cycle was commissioned by BBC Radio 3 for their 'Festival of the Violin' in 2002 as the text for Lyell Cresswell's *Concerto for Voice and Violin*. 'Cassandra' was commissioned by the BBC Scottish Symphony Orchestra for Cresswell's oratorio *Shadows Without Sun*.

Many of the poems have been broadcast in Britain and abroad: BBC World Service, BBC Radio 3, Radio Scotland, Radio Clyde, CBC (Canada), Mauritius Broadcasting Corporation.

The author would like to thank Edwin Morgan and Lionel Kelly for their help in selecting the poems, and the Scottish Arts Council for a most generous two-year Writer's Bursary which allowed him time to complete this book.

Contents

from *The Wonnerfu Warld o John Milton* (1974)

Invocation to Milton

Blin Milton poet, git tae it man!
gies somethin guid tae chow upon
- shair, a decasyllabic line impresses
specially whan it's got five stresses
risin and faain on thae even beats
we caa accentuated feets.
Ye were awfae clever maist o the time
- but whit a pity ye didnae rhyme!

Paradise Lost – The Hero

Whan the Deil moves he moves quick!
He's got style an speed an a slick
natter o patter wi his electric
accelerator flat-oot,
his tail flappin a fair lick!

He's a real fast mover!
Whit a groover! Hoover-sexed
he picks up every bit o fluff!
He's so far oot yin meenit – he's oot o sicht the next!
Yin warld's owre much fer him – but a thoosand's no enough!

Paradise Lost – A Summary

Book 1

It really cam doun tae a question o policy:
yin day Satan wis fair sick o His secrecy
an wanted a vote took
(he wis willin tae dae the coontin hissel, he said).
Then God gied him a richt fou blast o The Divine Look
an telt him tae get the Hell, which he did . . .
'An tak aa thae lefties whae're aye joukin roon an keepin hid
– they're owre lank an mealy-loookin tae be up tae ony guid!'

Book 2

Time passes an ward gits roun o God's plans
fer a new bit warld. Satan his a shaw o hauns,
coonts hissel the chief,
then feelin proper chuffed gangs fer a donner
tae see whit's daein – an gin aucht o yon reef
's real McKay he'll set an ponner
hou best tae scunner God. But God kens fine
that His Theory o Divine Grace is really Divine!

Afterward Remarks

An that's aa there is tae say, fer shairly
there's nae ither wey nou fer things tae gang:
were there a thoosand warlds an a hunner thoosand mair
'twad mak nae differin - afore lang
we maun stairt but whaure the last man leaves aff . . .
An gin we ever tear the hail jing-bang tae tatters
an dare face God Hissel we'll staun in Paradise,
but as afore a gless which gies aff
an image o oorsels reverse.
An wi anither mirror at oor back
we'd fill thon gless wi a thoosand warlds,
each yin a paradise tae mak
a hunner thoosand mair . . .
An gin the next man come an tear that aa apairt
then me and Milton baith oorsels
'll tak God's place an stairt
tae pit th'gither piece by piece
siccan image o Paradise as'll break yer hairt.

from *Stretto (1976)*

How Seagulls Move

Three gulls move circlewise
one between the other two
            and yet again
one between the other two

Their graceful paths close-bounded
trace such surface-tumbling curves
as would confuse the proofs
of circlewise Pythagoras

For planets move in harmony
and seagulls circle easily.

And so, holding the sun in my hands,
I watch the earth go spinning into the distance
– and consider how seagulls move.

Two Love Poems

The girl next-door caresses hersel in the dark:
she disnae hear the bedside clock tick:
but there's her quickenin breath,
an her hairt an her fingers an her lips,
till the birlin warld slips
frae her hauns . . .

Then she walks tae the windae an whispers her name,
fer the stars are like deils tae join in that game
where the heat o the sun and the chill o the moon
are the same.

★

Gless glinterin on the flair,
her bare feet stamp doon yince
an yince mair.

Then efterwards when scoorin oot the cuts
he'll kiss her only where it hurts.

A Bit Sonnet

Whae screives noo in this auld-fanglit style:
coontin yin an twa an three an fower an five
pair iambics, nae mair than alive
wi merchin pecht-oot in conscript rank an file
fer sonnet efter sonnet, a muckle trial
itsel withoot this up-doon jitter-jive
pentameteratin tae arrive
at half-wey hoose - an talkin sense the while?

Labbach

Owre an on, lichtlie an fou,
the years faa awa in a smirr as the caul
cuts tae the bane,
I staun as the wund blaws throu:

an owre an on, yont me ayont you,
the years faa awa like thunner like sun
the same frae the stairt,
I staun yerd-fast an I grue.

Withershins

The measure o the stars will never span
nor lichten yince yin glinterin meenit in the life o man,
but merks aff the oors an days an centuries lang syne
as gang withershins this life o mine.

Ootlins

Yin keek intae anither's saul
insooks the haill,
pullin every time an place intae yersel:

. . . clocks wind doon,
starsheen flauchters an gangs dim:

as ootlins o paradise we're yin
wi aa the craturs o hell
forbye that we micht love sae weel
anither saul's keethin.

In Memoriam Jimi Hendrix

Haudin the breidth an hecht o the universe
(the Deil at his richt haun, God at his left),

his fingers were gropin amang stars
fer the sichtless quasars
that boomed inside his heid.

Yin meenit ran a lifespan an back
as his hauns thrummled wi the years.
Yin weirdless keek an the warld couped . . .

An we're left whisperin tae oorsels
hou yince the planets circled us.

Pairty-Piece

Greta Garbo gies me ma tequila neat
'we've run oot o saut,' he says.
There's a blast o hell's heat
an angels whummlin aaweys.

I'm settled wi the bottle when
Greta's sister asks me whaure the hell I've been,
the pairty stairted lang syne, she's drouth
an wad I mind? She sits doun.

Mozart droons oot sixties' rock
frae the next room, there's a bit talk
wi Greta's sister aboot schuildays an soon
the music staps, the record clicks . . .

an time itsel sticks
as yin angel taks aff anither's claes
(she's leerin lovely wi her een)

'Play's anither tune,' she says
an roon an roon gangs Hendrix
a month afore he's deein,
birlin angels aaweys.

It's aa wummlin roon an roon ma heid,
this rummlin spate o heaven an hell,
while deils an angels turn insteid
tae burnt-oot stars lang syne deid

. . . an driftin machless as masel.

Shadows

Whit's wi us that gawk sae glaikit
at oor ain shadows?

Whit's wi us that tak it
wi a pinch o whitivver comes tae haun?

Gin I'm an eedjit
the warld's thrang wi owre mair that staun
toom-bellied an muckle-eened wi hope . . .

Whit's wi us that gawp
tae see oorsels as men? – syne
we're jist shadows flitterin on yin anither's een.

from *Creatures Tamed by Cruelty* (1979)

My Grandfather Dreams Twice of Flanders

My grandfather dreamt he was trying hard to die
and no one would help him.
He dreamt he went walking across Flanders field,
and he saw the companies of dead men
whose screaming he still hears night after night.

The countryside was a woman dressed in red.
He saw her courted briefly by a million men
carrying bayonets and mortars; her face
turning towards his, turned his to stone
and made the white clouds whirl dizzily overhead.

My grandfather dreamt that he was six years old
and a woman decked in flowers or blood
was guiding him to Flanders field:

he saw ungathered poppies scattered on the floor,
and the ceiling tilting crazily,
and the lights swaying.
Shadows tumbling out of the darkness beckoned him everywhere.

He saw her heaping flowers into a bed.
Then one by one she took the shadows
to lie with her, and one
by one he saw them disappear.

Elegy for Christine

She became birdsong trapped in the sky.
We became the earth where they buried her.

Listen to the sway of water-reeds,
the wind, the earth's breath,
to the river tearing this way and that to escape
whatever channel it's made for itself.

Listen to the songbird stabbed to the sky.

Poem for My Father

A flame shivers within me;
by its light I see hills, forests and cities,
the rest is darkness.

I haunt myself since childhood:
that solitary flame has cast each moment's shadow
as the heart's beat forces the moment on.

After he died, my father performed miracles.
He walks before me with his eyes closed
guiding me to other hills, other forests and cities
where I haunt those who live there.

Time and again his dead hand reaches for mine,
then I forget the laws of love and territory
and pass as helplessly through stone as through air
where he follows after, obliterating my path.

Seen by this trembling flame, the years are in disorder.
My father's become confused by so many shadows
circling the sky

that now he sees through my eyes:
seeking a world without light and without darkness,
to guide me there.

A Contemporary Interior

A woman is giving birth in the corner of the room

Let's listen instead to the sounds flowers make
swaying in the vase,
let's listen to the clock ticking in the photograph
sellotaped to the wall.

When these flowers burst into flame
we will let her new-born child play with fire,
when this clock strikes the hour
we will let him set its hands for all time.

Two Landscapes: Father and Son

My father becomes a forest without birdsong
where sometimes the wind keens in the high branches:
down here where I am
it is sunless and silent
until he dies.

*

A reflection on water where everything is
otherwise than it is:

Only where my shadow lies
do the sky and scale of things
seem accidental:

Every colour coming from the sun
resolves endlessly into an image
rising from the water

to become other than what's here
between my shadow and the sun,

resolving whatever accident I am.

The Fisher King

The fishermen shall be caught in nets,
their boats settle on the sea bed
where currents carry small shells drifting down
to litter the hulls, wheelhouses and holds.

Let them sit astride the roofs of their palaces and cathedrals
begging the moon to pull back the sea!

I shall walk the ocean floor as always,
remarking on life and death,
choosing now this and now that
as the glittering pleases.

Two Composers

I see everything by the light held
in my shadow's hand;
as I walk the candle-flame trembles.

Bach steadies everything, even light.

And the fields and woodlands I'll explore years later
become fields and woodlands now,
for moments at a time.

★

Mozart is very clear water
that seems only a few inches deep,
and yet you will never, never
touch the bottom

or, you will walk upon the surface
thinking that this is easy
and not the least miraculous.

The Colour of Bee-Sting

We faced each other across the kitchen table,
the shape of a very large field where we live,
– and just then your eyes took on
the colour of bee-sting.

As I reached towards you, I knocked over some wine
– and a host of small birds rose into the sky
taking with them the colours of the seasons
I had drenched red.

Then we sat in silence watching the sun
setting in the next room,
and waited for someone else to come
and hang up the moon by a thread.

A Lifetime

For twenty-eight years I have been watching these swans
rise into the air;
with their wings they beat the trees and the riverbank into pieces
as they lift themselves up.

You say that everything will be restored afterwards,
and it is taking you a lifetime to say this.

As the swans rise into the air I turn to kiss you,
but you are watching how the stone you have thrown
remains in the sky.

A Game for Adolescents

Let's you and I go down to the ice-covered lake
where the trees stand underwater.

'Come closer' you'll say as you climb up a slender silver-birch
towards certain death.

Minutes later you'll climb down dead
and unforgiving.

Meanwhile I've been watching the trees turn gradually
to silver-foil swaying in the current;

I've wrapped a strip of metal around these cold flowers
- take them!

Two Family Fictions

My mother and father are burning:

they rise from fire having brought me flowers.
They are trying to say they love me
but already their hands and tongues are flame.

I snatch their gift
then set the whole house ablaze

while walking unharmed from room to room.

★

The table is laid for me; in the centre
is a bowl of freshly painted fruit.

Something comes gliding into the room
through a crack in the ceiling,
and begins singing.

I see now that the crack in the ceiling
hides a crack in the sky
no smaller than a star.

The Colour of My Mother's Eyes

When I was eight years old I lived in a province
where Charlemagne's slightest wish was law,
and the woman I might have been
he made his empress.

For twelve hundred years we held court
among the dead men and the mad men:
seated side by side we stroked
any stray cat that came demanding power
– and to make the fighting cocks scream
how I'd clap and clap my beautiful hands!

He was overthrown one midsummer's day
– and as the rivers, woodlands, meadows and stonework
of the empire rushed into me, sunlight
crackled in my discarded clothes.

So do not ask me the colour of my mother's eyes:
for nowadays all I know for certain is
that while the exiled Charlemagne walks to and fro,
his courtiers amuse themselves with electricity,
making the dead jerk and the living scream
with laughter.

I Shall Show You Glittering Stones

I shall show you glittering stones
and creatures tamed by cruelty,
I shall say that they are formed
of light and darkness,
part image and part shadow
of yourself and myself:
- then you will become a forest or a lake,
or look lovingly at me through a woman's eyes.

I shall tell you that the sky
is the underbelly of a crouched animal
that tunnelled once upon a time into the daylight,
and that it stayed there
tense and afraid:
- then we will become whatever our embrace
can liken to ourselves

and to that creature as it turns upon us.

Anima

Whose face becomes hers whose lips kiss me tenderly?
Who is seducing me in the guise of this young girl?

Her eyes have been mutilated, they flick
from side to side,
and in her perfume I recognise the scent of - what?

Yet how I admire the skill her hands have
to confuse pleasure and pain, her body
and mine.

Woman and Music

She was half-come out of music
that I heard her form as breath:
the dark becoming shadow first
and the light distance.

So many, many is she
on all sides glittering and deep,
that excepting where she is
is darkness.

Her voice becoming echo first
and her touch remembrance,
that excepting where she is
is silence.

Then she becomes another woman and another
through the shifting light and darkness,
that I am hearing music still – though fainter now,
and more distant.

Surrounding Blue

My lover has returned, discarding
every colour she once wore . . .until
this surrounding blue.

I tremble to discover her again,
to hear her singing come from far,
far away.

Her fingers coarsen, grown more delicate for pleasure:
this measureless blue within her,
and beyond.

She is as Light Has Fashioned Her

She is as light has fashioned her:

My hands explore another and another darkness:

Neither touch, nor breath, nor echo, nor shadow:

Let the sun become a burning, burning rain!

List Number One

She is here always.

I have seen the other world: it is quite unlike a dream.

Our love is murdering our friends.

From the very first we recognised each other, the rest too will be a remembering.

Our friends died at the barricades. Their corpses are still lying there, yet even now we walk past them without discomfort.

Touching is like everything else love is.

My mother's heartbeat - then silence for twenty-three years.

I haunt my parents' house but cannot comfort them.

When I address her by name we are again meeting for the first time.

Love at second sight? We need a second chance to remember - at such times one forgets the past and the future, and the present.

We wait impatiently that we might remember everything.

Time doesn't stand still when we touch - it accelerates.

At the barricades they never sleep, or they sleep without dreaming, or they are dead. Those who fight are soon forgotten.

At the barricades there is no other world, only dreams and exhaustion.

The dead will never desert the barricades.

We kill and resurrect each other as each other.

The woman and magic:

List Number Two

The sun and the moon and myself: thus I have two shadows at all times.

Lovers cannot choose / to choose is to choose wrongly - but only the damned know this.

One shadow is defined and the other imperceptible / A past and a future, while I remain forever motionless in light, reflected light and darkness.

To love is to become yourself for the last time / Afterwards you will be echo and shadow of whatever daily circumstance you choose.

Not memories, but discarded alternatives.

Only pasts and futures alter, the present never changes / These shadows, the one lengthening and the other diminishing, comply with our every gesture.

She no longer resembles herself.

Only the damned see alternatives.

She casts a thousand different shadows and would choose them all / I have been living forever . . .

The sun above the moon, and on all sides a darkness completing her shadow and mine, resolving every past and future into this one horizon ablaze with light.

from *Ragtime in Unfamiliar Bars* (1985)

Descriptions of the Falling Snow

I described a flight of imaginary birds
across an imaginary sky in words
that played out every laboured game of skill
involving consonants and vowels, until
sufficient universal truths obeyed
the cadences of my trade.

I argued love and metaphysics through
by sound, resolving dissonance into
a line of formal spontaneity:
a passionate description of, let's say,
the falling snow. These were not dreams
but calculations for what seems

a well-constructed winter sky. Neatly
stammered syllables of discreetly
quantified despair described the view:
some fields of hardened grass and mud; a few
abandoned tractors; a waterfall's cascade
stiffening into ice. I made

events from over twenty years ago
translate into each metaphor – as though
a door slammed shut, or someone's name
had set the limits to my pain.
(And if the phrase read awkwardly I'd pause,
checking each effect for flaws.)

The qualities of light through falling snow;
the patterns made by frost; the fields below
my house – I scanned and stressed a thousand words
describing everything I saw. The birds
in flight across the imaginary skies
sang what I set down – my lies

were coming true. And yet, I cannot live
uncorrupted by the narrative
I tell. All things are mine to name?
There is no innocence, no shame?
Nothing is, that is not of my own
and of my incantation?

My fingers claw at imaginary birds.
My tongue stutters over lists of words
I've learnt by heart. Such passionate pretence!
Five o'clock – the day's work done, I sense
the hammer strike the bell and cancel out
each pitiless belief and doubt.

St Cloud in the Spring

Of the many versions of spring this one is mine
for the present: a suddenly coloured-in garden
beneath an imperfect blue sky, where inaccurate
songbirds keep changing their tune
as they fly round the sun . . .
                                        I lie and I wait
for my past to catch up – and it doesn't. I integrate
nothing, and nothing's omitted, and nothing's to come.

Let's welcome the droughts of November,
the snowfalls in June!

At Boulogne

It was almost raining when we met.
I remember concrete customs sheds, low cloud, wet
timber, a chilling sea-wind, a stack
of rusting tins, some black
grit heaped against a padlocked door.
Onto the watered-down shore
wash oiled sea-colours; the sky leaks
its weakest pigments, leaving streaks
the wind gathers and smears
across two frontiers.
A damp patch does for a horizon
where nothing is happening.

'The hovercraft seems rather late.'
Silence. I watch the sea evaporate
slowly; while several feet away
you ignore my opening remark. Its spontaneity
was well prepared. In lieu
of further preparation I repeat myself.
And so do you.

The November sun slides slowly upwards through
a greasy haze. A minute passes. Two
minutes pass. If it was still divine I'd pray,
but melting minerals and inert gases pay
such little heed to me. My mortal recipe
(two parts benevolence to three parts greed)
makes God, whether argued *a priori*
or seen in three instalments, less a certainty
than a Devil cloned to individual need.
For, with former dead, the latter's taken heed
and modernised: no messy blood-and-parchment now
but hi-tech psycho-system software. A silent vow,
computerised, will instantly allow
each man to choose his own temptation-terms. The old
Mephisto middle-men are out - damnation is controlled
directly by the sinner. No fuss, no queues, no pain.
Five million souls a second - and no last minute slips
of conscience . . . I hear what might be silicon chips
rattling in hell . . . All's well. I've sold
myself for just the right amount of rain

required to start a conversation.
I glance in your direction, smile, then casually unfold
my umbrella. I begin, 'Perhaps you'd care
to share my -' then stop right there.
Something's wrong. The air is growing warmer!
The Devil, perhaps confused by former
dealings - or thinking the bargain's bad - transmutes
the leaden clouds to gold.

My pea-green jacket with brown boots,
checkered shirt and flannels have already told
all Europe where I'm from. One moment's folly
has sometimes made our nation great:
I remark upon the change in weather, then hesitate
no longer, open out my British Brolly
to give, to both of us at once, complete
protection from the unexpected Continental Heat.

Great Moments in Scotland's History: Number 7

A ship lies gasping in the cupboard:
its crew disturbs my sleep night after night
with their demands to put to sea.

But no sooner do I close my eyes
and start imagining to myself the long ball
from Bruce Rioch that I take past one man, side-
flick past a second, and am lining up for a Peter Lorimer-
rocket-postage-stamp in the top right-hand corner
while the crowd goes wild, wild, wild
- when from behind the terraces I hear the opening strains
of the first of that evening's many sea-shanties.

I try to ignore it, and tell myself that back home
all Scotland's sitting boozed and bunneted in front of the TV,
watching me with only the goalie to beat
and the World Cup as good as on the mantelpiece.

But already the crowd's been infiltrated;
already some of them
(I suspect the ones with eye-patches,
and anchors over their shoulders)
have started singing 'Hearts of Oak'
in counterpoint to the crowd's roar
- and I see the goal-posts and netting sway gently
in an easterly breeze.

I try to ignore it for the ball's still at my feet
and I tell myself that back home
all Scotland's standing on the sofas and the sideboards
cheering themselves tartan.

But already the Easterly has freshened up,
the goal-posts are listing slightly
and, as the netting billows, are pulling away from the terraces
where *everyone's* now wearing an eye-patch
and has an anchor over his shoulder
- some of them are even watching the game through telescopes!

I try to ignore them and line up the ball for the big one,
the one that's going to be the one and only,
the most beautiful thing to come out of Scotland since McEwan's
Export,
the one they'll action-replay till the film falls apart.
The crowd gives out with 'Steady boys, steady!'
I try to ignore it
- the ball turns into a pink bobbing marker-buoy!
I try to ignore it
- the goals are towing the terraces of shantying sailors out to sea!
I try to ignore it:
Scotland's not going to be robbed, not this time!

Then suddenly I am alone in Argentina
No crowd, no ball, no goals, no cup.
The grass is turning to sea-water
- and it's a long swim home!

Two Variations on a Classical Theme

1.

When they awake it is midwinter: a London bedsit.,
floral curtains, iced-up windows - and for
the roaring surf at Delphos there's the hiss
of faulty central heating.
Next-door, a closet Monteverdi howls aloud
his breakfast madrigals and *canzonette*
in as many parts as he can manage while his kettle boils
drier than any *secco* recitative.

The Hero's triumph over death is symbolised
by simple gestures, stretching and the like,
performed with caution lest his touch suggest
awakening desire.
The Heroine lies still. She remembers nothing
of the songs that charmed her here last night,
only the rain upon a corrugated-iron roof,
hammering out applause after the final chorus.

They kiss awkwardly and feel obliged to give an encore.
There's the hiss of Stygian waters and, on cue,
the gondolier next-door begins to sound like Charon.
Terrified they'll lose one moment's tenderness,
her ghost and his mortality embrace.
Winter sunlight chills the room and lays
discoloured flowers, shuddering
at the slightest draught, upon them both.

Two players who have made up so often
their faces seem to shine with love
approach each other in the palace gardens.
Something has been arranged. Orpheus
begins to charm his way once more
with a clear conscience and a song.
Eurydice trails behind

stumbling among the props and deafening
effects – the stones, the wheels, the hiss
of accusation and desire.
Orpheus makes his way towards the wings
without a backward glance.
He sings of love, truth and beauty.

Though the palace is only three months old
Eurydice feels its pillars buckling at a touch;
she sees the tiled floor crack at each step
and the colours drain away.
Off-stage peacocks scream, or seem to.

She has nothing to say. With each lighting-change
a host of shadows lunge
and swoop around her, parodying
her exquisite and mute anxieties.

Until the very last moment Orpheus acts
without hesitation, and he mimes perfectly
whatever he leaves unsung.

The shadows slide into each other voluptuously:
which of these lovers will lead him out of Hell?

He turns to kiss Eurydice goodbye.

Indian Summer

As though time passes. Drenched in silver
and pale gold an ocean seems to break beneath us;
it brings together night and day imperfectly.

As though each sliding contour of the sky
has paused, the colours of the clouds
saturate the ocean.

As though it is a late September afternoon
we sit drinking wine outdoors; the dusklight falls
between our hands and soaks into the grass.

Soon moonlight will stain the ocean-floor:
sea-creatures will take fright
and turn away.

Night-Life

My nerves are stretched tight above the city:
a night-map of neon and sodium.

Hours earlier you wore darkness as love itself:
moonlight you ground more finely with each kiss,
starlight you scattered out of reach.

And now, what burning inside me?
what light trapped in a clenched sky?

The Philosopher Turns Accountant

I've listened long enough to those who state:
'Love needs no past or future; only *this*
is real; retrospective thoughts translate
but poorly into philosophic bliss;
that having kissed, the truly wise will let
the kisses go . . .' Their logic's fine, their premise
only I dispute, for none has met
or ever been in love with you
– or else he too
would free himself from wisdom, and growing yet
more wise, forget his theories, reminisce
most shamelessly as now I'm forced to do.

I live on your account, cross-tabulate
each item thus: your voice, your hair, your face
when smiling, perfume, touch. I calculate
your presence with these sad inventories,
converting their precious currency for private
circulation. Your absence is the base-rate.
I dream, imagine, appropriate
and hoard all such brief epiphanies.

My miserly affection will,
with love and metaphysical disgrace,
guide me well enough until
we can more cost-effectively embrace!

Mozart's Last Year

I picture him one summer's evening:
it's warm, he's seated by an open window
writing to Michael Puchberg. He's thirty-five years old:
a charming music-box they loved to praise and pass
from hand to hand in all the courts of Europe.

He's writing from the suburbs of Vienna, begging
for money. At night he dreams of Papageno:
he hears the bird-catcher's song while lime is shovelled
upon his upturned face.

Fellow-Travellers

Where timbrel, gong and drone sound invisibly;
where colours come only to those cuts of fruit
I dip into the spring and then to the patches of hard bark,
sand and the few slender stems I splash
in raising the fruit to my lips - there I drink deeply.

As the morning's heat sets the desert contours vibrating
so I - the more slow, the more dull with each mouthful of clear
                                                    water -
see between the several moments of the day,
between the certainties of hunger and thirst, slopes of soft sand
stretching to the distance. And between them,

between the shifting grains which a single breath of wind
could cause to cut me to the heart and make
my eyes weep, I see a fellow-traveller approach;
drawn, perhaps by the sound of unseen musicians
or the promise of water and fruit, to the same mirage.

Preparations for a Sea-Voyage

It was like this: we made the spare oars from wax,
the ropes from weed, smoke we gathered into sails,
and the prow was once the concentration of a cat.

After the embarkation party the doors
and hatches were slammed shut and screw-locked
- yet gatecrashers and their girls, their relatives
and their girls somehow barged in, promising to row.
We knew they never would. Instead we forced them onto all-fours
to scrub the decks, the cannons, the cannon-balls, the cabin-floors
and holds.
We gave them mops, pails and promises of rum,
then left them.

In time they finished off their chores.
They caught and scraped sea-creatures clean of phosphorescence.
(How the decks will shine at night!)
The mast, cut from the shortest distance
between two points sixty feet apart, they carved
and then inlaid with sea-tusk ivory and oyster-shell.
New arrangements of shanties, jigs and reels were made
and photocopied for the crew; they macraméd all the tangled ropes,
then neatly lettered each one through like rock: *In memoriam
all those lost at sea since Salamis.*
We expressed our thanks, suggested
they might form a chamber orchestra or leave. They left.

When our automatic pilot tracked down the setting sun
we cut the anchor free, and opened more champagne.
And now - full speed ahead!
I fear these oars and sails will not remain
as oars and sails for very long.

Letting Go

No longer a green orchard, nor blue;
for my hands are letting go
- even as you glance in my direction
my hands let go their jewels.

No longer an orchard nor the ocean
we saw surrounding us
- for even the taste of salt and grit are the same,
like sea-spray and precious stones.

Two Women

The room is stacked high with caged birds.
Feathers cover the floor.
One woman brings out tequila
while another, almost a child,
brings lemon, salt and a small sharp knife.

The old woman's songs are slovenly,
she makes herself cry. Then,
kicking up feathers, she makes the child dance through down-
drifting scarlet, vermilion and gold:
desert-colours for her lips, her breasts and her thighs;
the deadness of desert-light in her eyes.

Ragtime in Unfamiliar Bars

I'm teaching Peter how to play a suite
in the style of J.S. Bach, complete
with grace-notes. He suspects I improvise
the rules myself; I sit back, close my eyes
and bid him conscientiously repeat
each dreary trill. This exercise

can kill at least ten minutes. 'To modulate:
all keys and accidentals should relate
in your imagination *before* you play,
so take your time.' He's bored and doesn't pay
attention - yet he nods. 'Concentrate . . .'
He yawns.' . . . letting silence weigh

out sound as theme and counter-theme. 'Don't run
at it.' He shakes his head. I feel done-in.
Eleven minutes more and our release
will come; meanwhile, another masterpiece
to get through. The central heating's turned full on
I'm almost fast asleep. Grease

from Peter's lunchtime toast and tea covers
his fingers; keys stick; the score wavers
in the heat as bar-lines and breves macramé
tilting treble-clefs to weave in swami-
contemplations of their staves; quavers
are held fast in origami

tangles of tied-notes. My voice drones on.
Beyond the triple-glazing a winter sun
shines white, without heat, on snow. As if
to hear more clearly, garden plants stand stiff,
stripped down to their stalks and at attention,
antennaed for the slightest whiff

of J.S.B. - the perfect audience:
well-cultivated and without pretence!
Peter's too-abruptly phrased *allegro*
counterpoints my dull, tireless flow
of index-linked advice: 'and *four* . . . and sense
the beat . . . and *one* and *two* . . . and know

not only *when* - your metronome will show -
. . . and *three* . . . but *how* . . . Play each arpeggio
to modulate these weeks of diligence
into one moment's grace.' The dissonance
of *his* despair fits neatly in a row
of minor thirds. Adolescence

celebrates delicious and very private
harmonies - not music but intimate
sweet nothing sighed to soothe the pain.
And later, a composer? - A teaching-machine:
'Left-hand, right-hand, both together.' I hate
when they demand 'an easy nocturne',

- premeditated massacres, complete
with sighs, long silences and both their feet
upon the pedals! We sit like father and son?
like master and man more like! A buttered scone,
a cup of milky Earl Grey, discreet
I-won't-disturb-you smiles; this vision

of maternal tact then drifts next door
to strain the leaves again before she'll pour
more water in the pot. Double cream,
jam and powdered coconut redeem
her afternoon. Last week she asked: 'I'm sure
Peter's coming on a *dream* . . .

Has he begun on Brahms? Bach can be
so very dull at twelve, I'd hate to see
him bored. One doesn't like to interfere,
of course, but *Brahms!*' An hour's walk from here
my *Oratorio Profane* for three
hundred voices, children's choir

and pre-recorded tape rots in piles
upon the floor. De-structured parables
inter-cut Ecclesiastes; the last
words of Christ are Man's first - a vast
anti-fugue upon the syllables *Lama Sabachthani* cast

in twelve equal parts to symbolise
the tribes of Israel and the Serial cries
of Master Schoenberg wandering the Late
Romantic wilderness. I integrate
styles from Josquin, Ritter, Metz and Rheiz
to middle Boulez. There are eight

young Peters who must suffer for my art,
hating Czerny's 'School' as much by heart
as me by sight. Two 'Peteresses' tease:
while one caresses individual keys
and wants, she says, to let her fingers part
across an octave-stretch with ease,

the other giggles. 'Syncopation', 'touch',
'a fugal entry', 'not so fast', 'too much
for the desired effect' - they'll smirk and guess
a double-meaning. Their awkward gentleness
can almost break my heart. After such
a lesson I cannot work unless -

But who feigns interest in what I mean
unless my sufferings can intervene?
Sometimes I'll talk to strangers, get pissed and play
ragtime in unfamiliar bars. I'll stay
until the very end unless I've been
thrown out. I'll wander drunkenly

defying the empty streets to demonstrate
affection. The falling rain will delegate
for all creation. Enough! Peter's gone
already, and the piano lid's slammed down.
Scarf, coat, hat. The empty plate,
the cup and spoon returned. Upon

the table a folded ten-pound note I know
is mine. I take it and her thanks, then go
quickly from the house. At Peter's cry
I turn to see a snowman almost high
enough for Schubert. My oratorio
awaits, however - and so I wave goodbye.

Embroidery

I have laid your clothes out on our bed,
smoothing the lace, the silkand satin finery
seam by seam.

Only a mess of coloured thread
remains to fold away;
this embroidery you said was part-dream
and part-imaginary.

You would have finished it next spring.
These chalk-marks are clouds, and these – men fishing.

Before Leaving

Do you remember who made love an hour ago?
They lived for too short a time – and so

before leaving, I will pull you close:
your lips will press on mine
reprieving a lifetime, even
for the length of a kiss.

This Evening

You placed yellow roses by the window, then,
leaning forwards, began combing your red hair;
perhaps you were crying.
To make the distance less I turned away
and faced you across the earth's circumference.

The windowpane turns black:
across its flawed glass suddenly your image
runs on mine.
I stare at the vase until yellow
is no longer a colour, nor roses flowers.

The Night-Sky, the River and the Scent of Sycamore

While we talked long distance the night sky entered my room
and the St John river became a thick black line
drawn through trees and streetlights
- these were the elements of your voice.

Afterwards I stared at the parking-lot outside
while forcing the clock's hands months beyond
half-shut curtains, a print of Lake Niagara,
strip-lighting and an unmade bed.

I know these things are the clumsy antecedents of nothing:
your absence is all around me; and your nakedness
the scent of sycamore carried on the night air.

Above Saanen

If this were a country lit only by fragments of the sun,
a mountainside the colour of its flowers, how many colours
would I need were I describing *this,* above Saanen
- above its roofs, its streets and trees, its single-track railway?

If someone's hand pressed hard against my eyes, their voice demanding
'Guess who?' - whose name would I cry aloud while clutching
at the sound of running water, the cicada's noise,
or at a glider's silence passing overhead?

Pastureland and forest colours, dark green, red
and gold, establish early autumn.
Flower-light spreads across a darkened country,
emptying the sky.

A Love Story

The banisters slide up through the rain.
The woman cannot hold on, she slips backwards
into the waterfall.

The two of them struggle upstairs to their room,
to a broken skylight, a single-bar fire
and damp sheets.

Once upon a time he carried her all the way to the top.
Now she clutches at falling water
to pull herself up.

In A Japanese Girl's Room

You guided me through opium
while walking high above the streets of Tokyo.

You said, 'Let's enter this deserted building
and climb these stairs to the roof,
if no one's watching let's kiss.
Though it's too cold to undress
and too wet to lie down
let's make the best of it while we can.'

Then you said you would perform the tea-ceremony
as you had done for thousands of years;
and afterwards we undressed by candlelight,
and afterwards we lay in tears.

Elegy

You are lying in my arms more loved by me
than any woman I have ever known,
yet the fear of losing you has proved to be
my love's undoing. Each caress has shown
another source for our despair:
we touch and share the certain loss to come,
we snatch at time as at each colour
sunlight spills into our room.

Because we die each moment let us love the more,
and let love's metaphor be *resurrection*.

Restoration of a Painted City

The Clouds

The clouds were still drifting above Canaletto's Venice
when winter came.

They drifted into calculated sunlight
where they were coloured in.

They were photographed and made secure.

Our Room

The paintwork was so bare and badly cracked
we watched sunlight and moonlight
come shining through the walls.

When winter came our window was replaced
by a stroke of black paint.

The Acts of Restoration

The affairs of men and women are restored
to what they were two centuries ago.

The Grand Canal and quayside are scraped clear
of sea-fog and grime.

She sits at the mirror, making certain each smear
of make-up is perfectly in place.

She says she must return home. She tugs hard at strands of hair
– her eyes filling with tears.

Helplessly I list the possibilities:
That she will accompany the Doge's retinue;
That sunlight and moonlight will come shining through
our open window.
That the perfume she is wearing lingers;
That her fingers rest upon the kinsman's arm
whose skill at playing courtier will charm,
even with its silence, the silent Doge.

That those few moment's artistry with rouge
and lipstick will deceive two centuries' decay
– until another kiss creates another possibility.

The Embroidress

I watch her fingers busily stitch men and women
upon a roll of cloth.
I watch as they embrace in silence,
then slowly tear themselves apart.

For a moment she glances from her work
and beckons me towards her.
Her flesh and bone I breathe into myself,
her spirit settles on my lips and eyes.

Fascinated I watch my fingers working busily,
leaving a trail of men and women
upon a roll of cloth.

For too long I have been struggling with this dream
of endless stitching and endless mutilation:
everything depends upon the moment of awakening
– a moment that may have already passed.

Duet

The numbers, the colours and names that lay
in our hands were the music we soundlessly played
above hammers, levers and strings.

Our fingers were pressing down keys; they released,
as silence spanning one moment, the naming,
the counting and colouring-in

of all that we were, so briefly, just then.
What are the confusions of love, time
and despair - set against this?

A Gentle Demolition

Let us summon what real love there was
and free it now, before it is too late.
No conditions. Our rules and very private
statutes need repeal as every clause
at once turns advocate to plead the cause
of separation - urging us to hate
and so survive. We cannot legislate
and love, nor barter promises as laws.

And so, before we're forced to play the prison-
scenes of our particular despair,
that precedents and repetitious passion
will in time condemn us to, let's tear
this court-house down - a gentle demolition.
Then leave as friends, or lawyers, might - together.

Inheritance

Although there are nettles here, and thorns,
you will not be stung. Trust me. I've something
to show you made from twigs, bird-spittle, down
and journeyings in all weathers.

See how easily your hand covers the nest
and its eggs. How weightless they are.
Your fingernail, so very much smaller than mine,
can trace the delicate shell's blue veins until
they crack apart, letting silence spill
into your hand. There is a sense
of separation almost too great to bear . . .

Suddenly you long to crush all colour
from these pale blue eggs – in their brief
fragility you recognise as grief
the overwhelming tenderness you feel.
This is your inheritance:
your fist clenched on yolk and broken shell,
on fragments of an unfamiliar tense.

Claiming My Inheritance

I paused, then quickly tried to clear the mess
of yolk-slime and albumen. My distress
was private. I could not explain
what made me run home faster than
I'd ever run before.

Since then I've taken pains to learn
the language of what's done and said
(in restaurants, in stations, on the beach, in bed)
to friends (observing gender, number, business / social),
my fellow-guests, gods, the devil.
I've learnt the words for things and feelings: how and when
to use them. In making conversation,
love and enemies, I take especial care
no accent-lapse, no unfamiliar
tense construction, clumsy phrase
or hesitation (worst of all) betrays
I am a foreigner.

*

After I had crushed the eggs, a pause . . .

As if the colours of the earth and sky –

As if all the laws affirming spontaneity –

As if the present tense were happening too soon,
the fence I stood beside became a wooden thing.
the gate was iron-lengths – heated, hammered, bent
and riveted in place years earlier. I leant
against it. I struck it, but could not animate the dead
place to suffer for me. Instead,
the emptiness that stained
the empty sky above me blue,
gave definition to
my isolation.
Only this completed world remained.

The older I become the more
I am aware of exile, of longing for –
I clench my fist on nothing, and hold on.

My Inheritance

We've spent all afternoon in bed, hardly speaking.
Outside, a bird has begun to sing. Listen:

Since my father's death I've managed to disgrace
a dozen hearts and beds, making each a court
where I might love and talk of love, yet still support
whatever sinecures most pleasantly debase
true love into allegiance. Courtly etiquette
could make my servitude appear as *politesse*
– well-practised passion, warmth. I needed nakedness
to show my feelings, even to myself – to let
myself go. I parodied ingratiating
courtly roles: the tyrant seen deliberating
with cruel disinterest / the diplomat who's paid
to kiss away the pain / the fool who tumbles up
and down the stairs for some applause and won't believe
he's ever hurt (the show goes on because he'll stop
at nothing for a laugh – he's dangerous and mad,
needing an audience he's never last to leave).

*

My father's relatives were introduced to me:
they shook my hand and asked how I was getting on.
An aunt from Perth had made us sandwiches and tea;
her husband, talking of his crops, remarked that rain
would be the death of him. I laughed aloud but he
refused to see the joke. The relatives were shocked.
Earlier my father's corpse had been conveyed
from sight and burned. A shaky plastic screen had blocked
the view while Bach, beginning in mid-fugue, was played
to ease us through our grief. Afterwards we prayed.
Then Bach was pressed upon to serve once more
– a half-toccata saw us almost to the door.

Sorrow, deep regret, ten minutes' mourning-muzak,
silences and sympathy on double-time
plus tips. Electric motors jerked him quickly back
to an eternity whose span, with pantomime
precision, began just where a black-trimmed velveteen
conveyor-belt ran out. Everything had been

well-organised and went like clockwork, we looked on.
The lodger drove us home.

                           Ten years ago today
my life began by launching Father down that slipway
to unsounded oceans' measureless mirage.
Champagne against the coffin-sides! Bon Voyage!
Call up unearthly winds to speed his odyssey
among the kingdoms of the dead. An embarkation
service said in Greek to keep the Classic tone.
I slaughtered bulls, burnt thigh-bones wrapped in fat, the slow
uncoiling smoke I read for signs while letting flow
my filial tears unchecked *etcetera, etcetera* . . .

Since then whatever I might wish to do
seems scarcely mine, but is at once anticipated
by a sense of his return. Ten years seen through
one imagined moment. In time, the ghosts
and demons we create from nothing to share
our loneliness, become our overlords. These hosts
of our invisibility demand our blood
to let them speak. My father's spirit cries aloud,
claiming back the life he gave me - and I, his creature,
cling even to my despair.

                  All my subtle thoughts have led
only to subtler thoughts. Like Penelope
forced to stay behind, I weave each hated thread
into its rightful place, then tear the tapestry
apart, dreaming I cancel out my grief. Instead,
some stars have been displaced, distant oceans spread
elsewhere, and then denied. Alone, I celebrate
both love and loss of love together in one image
of desperation. Dream-suitors come to me. They state
conditions for my next imaginary marriage:
they strip the gardens, fields and cellars; they desecrate
the family shrines; they force me to adjudicate
their drunken games. When seasons meet in me as darkness
- then hatred and desire are all I need to bless
my dream-adulteries.

If I would live, then I must suffer *everything* I am. The dead
are not responsible for me - they cannot give
a little meaning to my life. I have paid
for my inheritance with all I have - the price
is fixed at that, and I must settle for nothing less
if I would live and be myself. I am afraid
to bargain with the dead, but must do. Dreams betray
this world's a metaphor come true
and incorruptible - Time foreshortens to
a gesture of ambiguous delay.

★

When you and I make love we enter silence:
the noise of kings, courtiers and fools
does not reach us here. Sincerity, pretence
and tact lose meaning; established courtly rules
are valueless. We kiss and kiss again, as though
caresses have so weighted down Time we know
whatever is - is ours; and every tense
becomes a plaything we can share.

Listen to the singing outside our bedroom window:
such singing is all the world - and trapped out there.

from *Histories of Desire* (1995)

At Linton Kirk

Linton Kirk is stone and timber hollowed out of air;
where stained glass darkening to shadow traces out
a present tense across the floor.

Our first weekend together: a night without much sleep,
a morning's levitation over hills and cold rain.
The visitor's book lies open. We flip the pages back
to catch sight of a world before we'd met,
then pause uncertain what to write. I glance outside:

an east wind scours the burnt yellow fields to black,
tearing colours from trees; the blunted edge of winter sunlight
hacks at names, dates and words of consolation;
the dead withdraw into the living.

Your scent, the blue-and-silver patterned scarf you wear,
our closeness - these are not memories.
Once we've signed the book and put the date we'll leave
and Linton Kirk stand empty.
How far into the future can I reach to take your hand?

Creation of the World

An ocean hardens into Linton valley as line
on line the winter geese fly south, tidemarks
reaching to a farther shore.

The ocean's freezing over: wind scratching its surface
here and there suggests what might have been.
Someone's voice, another's glance, the taste a woman's skin has
as she wakes – all these remain and are
the brittleness of shells.

The geese trail silence after them until the shoreline
disappears. This is the ground we stand on
– dark sand and darker water.

A rowan tree takes root beside our house;
a stone bridge hump-backs over Linton burn;
the hill we'd planned to walk across today
is turning green. Creation of the world seems easier
than a change of heart.

Near Linton Burnfoot

Tarred roads, metal cattle-grids and wheel tracks mesh
so tightly no land can escape; tractor ruts
cut deep into the grass to cross and double-stitch
the fields together; where the high ground pushes upwards,
pylons rigid with electricity stand guard
upon the hills. Bridges staple running water,
lines of fence-posts nail the valley sides in place.

Rain and ploughed mud. Rooks' cries claw the air;
a *banshee* trapped in corrugated iron shrieks
to be released. Trees grasp at nothing and let go –
a thousand masts rammed deep into one deck, and yet
the countryside remains becalmed. It is a scene
a child has painted, splashing colours on sodden paper:
his carelessness might tear a mountainside apart.

Shingle being ground to nothing on the river-bed,
the clouds' silence soaking into the hills –
these are secrets I dare not tell
even to myself. They weight each moment of my life.

Coming of Age

You're waiting for a train that isn't late,
or glancing out the window at the street
before the curtain's pulled.

Some broken glass, a child's ball bouncing
down a flight of steps, the threat of
rain, a ploughed field,
the colour of a passing car
- each in turn betrays the man you are.

Take care, your heartbeat's stilled
and still you do not die. No delegate
can take *your* place or answer to *your* name:
when the curtain's closed the world's shut out.
Your train arrives on time.

Histories of Desire

That was when I threw the stone and then ran after;
splashing into Smallholme Burn I made the colours
of a summer's day cascade around me.
That was when the water stilled to rowanberries, clouds
and dark green leaves I could never reach before.
I tried to pick one up –
that was when the earth and sky first slipped
between my fingers.

All histories are histories of desire, they tell me
how my life begins and ends: a stretch of water,
a stone a child sends skimming
to the other side.

The Start of the Affair

Let's tear the moon in half and keep the darker side.
Turn out the light.

(Shadows of a man and woman touch and then let go
– these, the only truths they know,
are trapped between the only words they dare not say.)

Turn out the light, but do not turn away.
One fragment of the moon brings night,
its ragged light is all we have to see by.

Flic-en-Flac

A yellow bird pecks at Mauritius island, then flies off.
The concrete paddle-steamer we're staying in has run aground.
The jungle round us has been cleared for re-flotation, for litter
and mosquito pools of rain.

Our half-completed steamboat (minus paddlewheel
and smokestack) has sunk up to its windowsills
in sand. With land values rising by 50% per annum,
it's a voyage of pure speculation.

We spend our evenings small-game hunting in our room.
Every morning we rediscover red, gold, green
and silver-striped fish browsing upon the silence
of underwater trees.

Midday, the smallest particle of the sun breaks off
to settle once again upon its own shadow. *Peck-peck-
peck* while twenty yards away the jungle rots, feeds
and grows without harvest, without season.

One Life

Once when he was young he reached into the fire,
longing to possess the colours there.

He is the fire he reaches into now.
Grasping at flames, he burns.

He is the colours that one by one return.

Our Last Night in Africa
(for Randall)

I bargain for an inch-high king,
his queen, their servants and musicians worked
in bronze. *A good price for you, my friend.*
Special good price.
The souvenir that I've been looking for.

Night curtains off the whole of Africa
with one quick tug.

Insects hiss us back to our hotel.

We wash, eat. An old man shuffles to our table
when the prostitutes give up.
Onto the heavy linen cloth (the only green
we've seen for days) he lays a clumsy-looking bangle,
inviting us to feel its weight.
See, my gentlemen, please see.
He sits for almost an hour and hardly speaks:
there are no words for where his village used to stand;
none for how the sun became imprisoned in him,
and will not rise.

★

Our fan is broken. I cannot sleep. I've come downstairs:
the fountain's been switched off, the plastic chairs are stacked
in silhouette, the electricity's cut.
Still-life: 'Central Hotel, Kano (only a taxi-ride from the Sahara)'.
The courtyard's breathless heat and darkness
sketched in as moonlight
(that same shade of metal-grey the old man placed
before us). This after-tint reveals the hidden detail:
the line of men, women and children,
each one with a bangle hammered
to their wrist . . .

Our last night in Africa.

Rubbing out the moon, I find what's nailed there
in its place.

African Sunlight

A man is riding a slender camel, a woman
carrying a jar - two lives that give a human scale
to the empty landscape and open skies.
Their faces lack expression. Unspoken lies
suggest a husband with his wife,
a king and his slave, strangers even.
The jar she offers him contains cold water
tasting of exhaustion or desire:
the words of greeting he will never speak
will never bring her peace.

The artist threads his needle, pulls tight,
bites off what isn't needed, spits
and then begins upon the same two lives again.
Beneath his fingers the wax-embroidered sun remains at noon;
the desert sand raised up as darkness, catches fire.

Prayer

When I reach the centre of the earth
let there be someone with me.
All things must bear the world's weight,
but not alone.

So when I return at last to this same hour
and this same place,
let there be someone raising
even the emptiness in their hands towards me.

Budapest: All Wars Are Civil Wars

The unfamiliar names of things soon blur
when I'm alone. I'm standing on a balcony;
nearby a church bell sounds the hour's surrender.
It's evening. History clings to every moment here:
bullets, hand grenades and mortar-shells
have gouged their foreign script into the walls.

The Earth is tilting further from the sun
till east and west are forced into the one same
shadow. Night divides into a map of years
whose territories are now the street below
reaching to the far side of the world.
I stretch my hand into the dark to greet
whoever's there.

All things stand everywhere complete:
the church bell's silence marks a pause
between the past and future;
I touch the Earth and feel its weight.

Don Juan at Forty

There isn't time for every clip-on bow
and straight. You're late. Wait –
and you'll get left behind.
Accelerate –
or die. Now, pick a tie.
But not that cross-check wreck – you blind?
Your new shirt's double-fluted ripples flow
against it; tartan's even worse. You'd like to wear
the birthday cufflinks, centre-part your hair,
risk the two-tone shoes? OK, then choose. And no
half measures. You've reached your fortieth year –
it's time to put your trousers on, and show
the world who's master here.

Another tie? Let's try this Paisley-patterned swirl
of calloused colours, curves and broken nerves –
and knot it tight. Here's the mirror. Right: full-frontal/
profile. *Tighter.* The birthday-boy deserves
the birthday-best. That's *your* reflection pressed against the glass
– press back to steady it. Such moments pass.
Ready? Deep breath, chest out, turn, step *one*
and *two* and *three.* The door. The landing. Stairs.
Breathe deeper. Good, now grip the rail – and *ten* – don't run
– *eleven, twelve* – let go the rail – and there's
your guests assembled. Smile. It's time to mingle,
picking out which women might be single.

Cough for silence. Speech. Your few words say
how deeply moved you are: that done you turn away.
Romantic overtures for two, played by ear,
begin: you know the score by heart and sound sincere
even to yourself. Your grace-notes whisper sweet,
sweet nothings. Only lesser artists need deceive
– what *you* say becomes at once what you believe.

Look across into the mirror, there:
Don Juan at forty, the man with thinning hair,
in syncopation with himself alone,
a virtuoso doomed to solo on
and on towards the loneliest harmonic . . .
But see, he's found a partner, modulated into tonic

doubling on gin to toast their new duet
(set in two-part harmony to let
his smiles and well-timed glances emphasise
the hidden theme). His heartbeat bass-line plays
its two-note phrase *staccato* as he lays
a hand upon her arm. He talks: he tries
'philosophy', then 'feelings'. What's left unsaid
suggests a taxi home, more drinks, then bed.

But here's a husband. Smile. Firm handshake, birthday
greetings tendered and accepted. Once more
the whole world's someone else's wife - her sympathy
and closeness starved by you into desire.
More drinks. Let's offer round the tray of cheese-squares,
dips and olives - the picked-at sticks and stones
are worth a joke about mortality.

★

After midnight and alone. You still have time to part
the curtains, stare into the dark, possess the stars
- their distant chillness cannot touch your heart
for long. So lock the windows, doors, the bolts and bars,
snib what can be snibbed. If not love,
then some remembrance of who you are endures
- without, each man condemns himself to prove
the dreams he lives by. These dreams are yours:
they dress you, move your right foot forward,
then your left, prompt your every word . . .

Here is your empty bed.
Switch off the light and do not be afraid.

What I Remember Most

Your heart was the given heart.

Mine had long ago been hammered into place.

We listened, pretending the beats were counting out *one life, one life, one life* . . .

★

10am, and we were still awake.
Morning couldn't reach us. Our love-heat,
that mist upon the windows, had stopped the sun
from entering your room.

★

Since you've asked, I'll tell you what I remember most:

We're dressed. We're standing close together. It's time I left.
I feel the usual awkwardness, and wish
we'd kissed goodbye already and I'd gone
– for that is how our past anticipates, is lived out
and a life is done.
Just then you give the steamed-up glass a wipe
to clear it. This could be my chance:

A show of wounded feelings, shocked politeness.
I'll tell you that our night is not to be so easily erased.
Not for me at least.
The perfect exit line, then off.
I'm ready to deliver when you catch my eye
– you're smiling.

A moment's misunderstanding, you might say
– but it had lasted all my life.

You have to place your hand upon my shoulder.
You have to turn me round to make me look again.
How long until I understand,
and feel my heart breaking, at last?

For that's what I remember most: your given heart,
and mine released to see the busy street outside,
to see the city where we now live.

The Lake at Preda

The stream has ended in a glacier-green transparency of cloud,
blue sky and mountain shadow. We sit down,
we share our wedding-breakfast listening to the water's rush
become accumulated stillness.

When we return next winter the stream will have been silenced into
ice.
This lake, the scene of our true wedding, will be a sounding-board
set between high mountains
– safe enough to stand on, jump on, dance on.

When we return – what music we will make!

Advertisement for a Scottish Servant

Would you like a very Scottish servant all your own
who'll do for, spiritually speaking, you alone?
A lad o' pairts: a prophet, historian and more,
a therapist/composer who understands the score?
Guaranteed - your past and future contrapuntally combined
into a pre-determined present so defined
you'll never need to think or feel again!

Your gardener for life, his motto: prune first, then restrain
the slightest sign of growth. He'll cut you down to size
(for your own good), then train your roots to do
their darkest: dig deep, grasp, immobilise;
if needs be, split your soul in two.
He'll anticipate your every beck and call
- he *kent yer faither,* after all!

As a Scottish-school economist he takes great pains
where pain was never due. No credit-giving Keynes,
he soon has Adam Smith's close-fistedness outclassed,
insisting every childhood trauma last
your lifetime. All you'll need to know is what he'll tell you,
even when you're sleeping he'll compel you
to treat his dreams as if they were your own.

Say 'Yes' - he's yours! Your very own: flesh, blood and bone
passed on as Scottish fathers pass him on
to Scottish sons (with references supplied
unto the seventh generation). A tendency to patricide
but nothing serious - just words - so never heed him.
This very Scottish servant - do we really need him?

The Shadow-Sailor

He's quite at sea *(that,* at least, is true).
By day he plays the captain and the crew
with rank and medals tattooed on
- gentle pinpricks cutting to the bone.
By night the empty crow's nest sways
between the cold moon and himself, and weighs
out stillness for the darkened scene below,
letting the slightest measure only, flow
into his sea-crazed mind.

A tightened grip upon the helm and steering blind
he navigates by willpower, shapes
the changing waves according to a map
long out of date and precious. Ink-blots, tears and scrawls
mean 'Danger - hidden reef', and 'wreckage'.
Sea-wraiths and the demons who preside
upon the ocean floor advise him. Their histories
are his, their voices he alone can hear
- their silence, his despair.
And so his world has taken shape:
a place of terror, clashing rocks, the hiss
of cross-run currents, undertows to rip
his soul apart. Ghost-ships glide
through his, each unsounded passage falls
shadowless across his decks and hull.
He shuts his eyes to ward off the invisible.

★

He's more than halfway round his lifetime's only world:
to north and south the cries of drowning men have turned to ice;
to east and west the ocean and the sun
dissolve into each other.

It's time to voyage further: to see what lies
beyond this shadow-sea, these shadow-skies.

It's time to take into himself the heavens'
own creation and destruction:

to make, of stars and minerals,
the darkness his imagination spills
unearthly light upon.

71

Edinburgh: A Place of My Own

If I had sat outside the Caledonian Hotel
this afternoon, cross-legged on the pavement,
with the restaurant wall behind me -

If I had placed a plastic cup in front of me
and a blanket round
my shoulders -

If the hours had been the east wind cutting
the length of Lothian Road, while
the cold hardened into me -

If the day could not have been different, or the date
or the clouds or the sleet
or the rain -

If I'd stopped looking round me at faces,
at people; if I'd stopped staring down
at my uncovered hands -

If I had been sitting up straight
when they asked me to move -

If I'd still been sitting up straight when they touched
my shoulders to wake me -

★

A woman. A plastic cup. A blanket.
The pavement.
The wall.

They told her she had to move on.
She said nothing.
They asked her her name.
She said nothing.

★

If a sheet had been used to cover my face -
If the post-code for where I'd been begging
were tagged to my foot -

That post-code would stand for my name
when, at last, I'd be given a place of my own.

Three Biographies

This morning. The weather. The bus. What is outside
is out of focus: the Clerk Street shops are blown across
the glass as rain; traffic-lights smear.

A man's hand touches the side of his face
every few seconds. Next to him
a girl, whose fair hair's much too short
to be comfortably looked at, chews
and stares. Next again, is me.

Three biographies all up to date:
we turn the page, read on (our dreams alone
our own responsibility).

The traffic stops. It's dark enough to see my likeness
looking in: mid-forties grey to silver-
grey. He's caught my eye.

He'd like to smile, and does;
he'd like to reach his hand towards mine,
make contact. Be *sure*.

★

There are spirits trapped outside us;
we keep them at arm's length or
beyond. Their image caught on glass:
a spell conjuring who we are
as if from nothing; and our lives
the small enchantment that remains.

What we know is what we fear we have to lose.
No mark upon the man's skin,
no sign of pain . . .
The girl's nailed-in hair,
her hands' stillness, her perfume.

What we fear is what we know will break the spell.
The bus jerks forwards: Clerk Street,
the rain, the filthy window.

Our histories continue out of sight.

The Landscape We Live In

There is no bridge, there is no river –

The path no longer reaches to the hill –

The silver birch becomes a clutch of splintered branches –

Above us, a bird has paused with its wings outstretched.
How long before the sun itself ceases to move
unless we force it?

Lifeline

A certain woman takes my hand in hers to trace,
as best she can, the lines (some broken, some
complete) upon my skin. Signs, she tells me,
of the man I have become.

For the first time in my life I flinch in pain –
this open wound slashed long ago
across my palm.

A Final Word on the Dream-House

Here is the house I lived in once: another man's house,
another man's dream.

These are the rooms that obeyed him. The corridor's length
is witness to the tone he spoke in;
the banister rail is edged with sunlight – his knuckles clenching
to holding his dream-house together.

Only those we've forgiven can die.
Let this be the final word on the dream-house.

Day and Night

By day, my heart's a language I cannot speak.
My house is exile. Here is my empty hand,
here is where I next draw breath.

By night, we find stars set in our hair,
in our eyes, in our skin
– and cannot stop the darkness rushing in.

Barcelona: August 10th

Sunlight scours the terrace where I'm sitting.

I speak your name aloud, expecting – what?
You are not here, nor ever coming here.

Love alters nothing but ourselves.

I want to raise my hand in farewell, nothing more.
Surely I do not have to move the sun
to mark a new beginning?

Adult Education

The young boy's fingerprints smear
the falling rain, then prod a river into place.
He smiles: 'Your turn now.'

Thumbs first, so as not to make a mess, I press a set of ten neat
                                                                circles
endlessly shut in, across the page.

He shakes his head, tilts the paper to let the colours run,
then takes my hand in his:

At my fingertips he shows me unknown solar systems spinning
into unknown skies, and whirlpools
roaring to the centre of the earth.

Letting the Demons Speak
(for Roger, and Anja)

1. *The Carry-out Calendar*

The usual picture: two Chinese men, a tea-house,
a path, a mountain with its cloud (top right) as if
to post the early evening far into the future.

No background, but then there never is.
The unpainted parts between the tea-house
and the mountain, the mountain

and the cloud, remind us (once
we've phoned our order in, of course,
and have to wait

and wait) of how the infinite surrounds
man's every moment, or the eternal
something...

Anja-Time, that metaphysics of canine greed complemented
by complete forgiveness, repeats one life
over between sleeps.

Two bottles and sufficient cognac will remove the background
to *our* evening also: every top-up helps us
paint out a little more.

That's where the demons are: hiding just beyond the first,
the second and every glass, and coming nearer;
re-shaping Time into a series of concentric moments set
to trap us at the centre.

Elsewhere, the Scottish Tao: Say nothing
until you're sure it is too late;
Do nothing until you're sure there's nothing
can be done. The Scottish Way is - no way.

And so, two Scottish men, two Chinese men,
twelve hundred years apart, sit down together
to let the demons speak.

2. *Anja*

Thursday evening. 6pm. Anja barks the flat into an urgency:

The streetdoor's banging shut is followed once,
twice,
thrice,
      by the faintest.
                    then less faint . . .
                                  step
                                        by
  step
                                    as every step
                        proves . . .
                not . . .
          to be . . .
      the last:

Three floors down the messenger begins his 47-stair ascent - and
Anja *knows*.

                          ★

(Once upon a time she visited the Eastern Pearl:
Its door pushed open, she entered no longer walking
upon the surface of the earth . . .

As we left, she barked to the effect that our departure was,
essentially, a banishment, a return to Plato's cave.
The shadow-crackers cooling in the plastic bag would taste,
she added, of exile and greater longing.)

                          ★

She cannot wait for lesser beings' single speed to catch her up:

She herds the slowest seconds into a flock:
She barks them
She whines them
                        She harries them around
the table legs and chairs
She chases them into the hall
     Clockwise
                            round the brolly stand and back
             until they're penned in
        and done with
instantly.

She's at the door now, glaring across the gap between us
and the future she's already reached *(there,*
the bell's been rung, the meal delivered and is being shared).

3. *My friend and I*

The two of us meanwhile (too-human, therefore trapped
in a continuum of four dimensions seen as three)
must plod our one way at our one speed
towards the worktop and the draining-board (landmarks
on our journey through time)
collecting souvenirs, arranging them
(these articles of our remaining faith in any remaining future)
upon the kitchen table: the plates, the bowls, chopsticks,
wine, the Chinese teapot, napkins, place-mats,
glasses, cups.

The corkscrew.

★

The doorbell rings. The Eastern Pearl delivery resolves
both dog-barked time and our conventional delay.
We pay. Unwrap.
Sit down.

The demons would prefer we gossiped, talked politics
or art (three very demon-topics
certainly discussed in ancient China).

Gossip: Speaking of someone else's pain to ease our own.

Politics: Our deepest fears recycled as conviction.

Art: Renouncing our demons and ourselves, briefly.

Instead: Some Opus 20 Haydn, spring rolls and the first Rioja.

4. *The Meal Begins*

There are no demons in the tea-house, at least
none visible. The bamboo door's slid open: one man's leaning

forward as if to stress a point he's made, or hear
exactly what's been said. The other's attitude remains

unclear: he's been badly printed, no more
than a smudge across the table.

(Anja's no dog-noun any more. A mouth, a highly active verb
beneath the table: *Waiting.*

An alertness of fur and ear and eye: *Stretching*

towards a truth so far beyond us
as to taste of blasphemy . . .

For her, the here and now's restored as one,

                            two,

          three,

gobbled-down crackers)

My friend sits opposite; nearby a second bottle breathes
on our behalf. The pause between two Haydn movements sets
a frame of sudden silence round us:

Brushstrokes never made upon the invisibility of silk
show us all that is not here, and all
that is – within the clenching of our hearts.

Elsewhere, metaphor and imitation: nothing in our lives
accepted merely for what it is, ourselves included.
Elsewhere, the telephone rings, a letter arrives –
we grow older and more afraid.

So, more wine, another aluminium trough of lemon chicken!
Here come the demons.
Welcome.

Ryecroft
(in memory of my mother)

1. *Departures*

My mother died much slower than expected:
I saw her, talked, held her hands, sat,
held her hands, kissed goodbye
and left the nursing home. That visit lasted seven months.

Soon it will be March. We have returned to work on Ryecroft:
a front door of hardwood panels crumbling
to yellow dampness;
a backdoor of corrugated metal hammered
onto rotten planks.
The window frames and ceilings are secured by clouded stillness
gathered into filth around the bundled-up dead.
Uncurtained daylight chills me.

There has been no winter until now:
a bedroom already hardened into ice around
a hairbrush, comb, kleenex, photographs and her stiffening
face upon the pillow.

2. *Beginnings*

Destruction must come first, and second and third:
a chisel and steel toe-caps to the sagging floors and skirting;
a sledgehammer to the fireplace whose brickwork flinches
when it's touched;
bare hands to the ribcage laths and plaster.
Everything shovelled up and wheelbarrowed outside.

2174 slates are stripped off: a century's darkness lifts
for an afternoon. There's the slightest catch of breath
as every one of 2174 nails is drawn out.
The skylight, a bloodshot and corroded eye rusted half open,
is plucked out with a crowbar.

The garden (on neighbourly advice) will be poisoned
into submission.

3. *Walking Together*

Before my mother starts her journey home
she has to rest a moment:
last week we reached the fence beside the railway line,
today we've come no further than the yellow bush.

When I feel her touch upon my arm I know
she's ready to turn back. She doesn't smile:
grasping her stick as tightly as she can she moves
forwards, testing the ground at every step.

4. *The Rats*

Their sky was laid out in planks with hardly a Rizla-paper's gap
between each tongue and groove. Underneath,
a black sea without tide, night without day;
where the floor was badly wormholed stars began. Is this
the rats' astronomy? Does the rate of wood decay
when set against the lifespan of a rat, allow
a glimpse of the eternal?

Those who've read their futures in the wormwood
have hurriedly moved on; the rest will see the light too late.
A firm tug. The lino lifts. New heavens blaze above them . . .

Afterwards I hammer-claw the lengths of sky for burning:
the rustiest nails snap cleanly;
the best - Excaliburs eased out in one.

5. *This year*

As the days grew shorter we'd sing our way home through darkness-
her voice in front, mine half a step behind.
Trees clawed at us and the wind hissed -
I held her coat tight.

This year we keep to the concrete path around the building.
Tea and biscuits in her room. A bed, a chair, radio,
some photographs; she says she's everything she needs.

Another day has passed, another evening. I'll leave soon.
I have to. When the trees press too close our hands touch:

There is no singing, no road home.

6. *The Bath*

Standing in the middle of a field: claw-footed,
white-lipped, porcelain-plungered, fully stretched
for the reading of detective novels in;
ocean-going, and of Jurassic proportions
all but extinct in this designer-world.

Less than two miles from the river Annan. There was mud
to walk through, thistles, nettles and cows to avoid;
barbed wire to climb over. A cloudless sky:
the sun had a perfect view of me the day
I first climbed in, trying it for size.

7 *The Curtains Were Closed*

The curtains were closed when I entered your room:
the day was shut out, the night was shut out
and you weren't there.

I looked down at your face, your mouth and your eyes:
I tried to remember your mouth and your eyes.

The walls were as mist when mist disappears,
the door falling rain that no longer falls;

the corridor ran the length of the world
and you weren't there.

8. *Clambering Up*

These rafters, dirt and cobwebs will be turned
to sunlight on varnished wood.
No staircase yet. I'll help you clamber up.
I'll fight off spiders.

The trapdoor hinge sticks. Wrenching the metal back
I touch the coldness of my mother's hand.
I feel her fingers claw the air in front of her.
I kneel beside her bed until her weightlessness becomes

your smile, your red hair drawn up into my arms a moment past.
This is the beginning of winter and of spring.
We pause for breath. In dreams alone there is finality:
I hold you both as tightly as I can.

Absinthe with Eddie

There's an age that people get stuck at.
(Some of my schoolfriends were already forty,
and still are; others hit adolescence once,
and never moved on.)

You're different. You're younger than when we first met
a generation ago. While the rest of us have been taking good hold
of the passing years, turning them into something solid
and durable around us – to keep the world out
and ourselves trapped safely in – you've been dismantling Time
and Space into words, sounds and silences. . .

Some friends and I paid you a visit recently.
Lunch over, you prepared an afternoon tray of glasses
and illegal absinthe. You invited us
to *go on, give it a try* –

When I picture you now, I picture you smiling:
in every poem, you're offering us the unexpected taste
of Life itself – as something altogether new,
and ours for the having.

A Recipe for Whisky

Wring the Scottish rain clouds dry;
Take sleet, the driving snow, the hail;
Winter twilight; the summer's sun slowed down
to pearl-sheen dusk on hillsides, city-roofs,
on lochs at midnight.
And, most of all, take the years that have already run
to dust, the dust we spill behind us . . .

All this, distill. And cask. And wait.
The senselessness of human things resolves
to who we are - our present fate.
Let's taste, let's savour and enjoy.
Let's share once more.
Another glass for absent friends. Pour
until the bottle's done.

Here's life! Here's courage to go on!

A History of the Scottish Parliament
(for Rhona Brankin)

God's first week was a busy one:
universal chaos, light and darkness, stars, planets
and attendant moons (the Divine Breath occasionally
lending atmosphere), oceans, continents and so on . . .
Come Sunday He stayed in bed.

Time (that shove of Divine Encouragement, turning
what might otherwise have stayed a hobby
into something with a future) began to pass.
The senseless destiny of things took up more and more Space. Life,
and then death – all in the blink of an innocent eye.

Counting backwards through the tribes of Israel's begats
and begones, Bishop Ussher dated God's Last Laugh
at 4004 B.C. The rest is history.
Fast forward through that blur of good and bad intentions
(the fewer taking part the better

chance for love) to Scotland, 1999.
We vote, we count. Peter Pan and Wendy grow up
overnight. They're forced to. Sudden though –
no adolescence, no trying out new looks, new styles,
new attitudes. No chance to practise who they are.

Instead, from Day One: a house of their very own,
a job, a diary to be filled. Adult responsibilities.
Then two houses, then three: one borrowed from the church;
one standing empty (are they expected to return to school?).
The third's a *concept*, like 'the future'

(that darkest continent at whose borders we fret
away our lives), like 'National Identity'.
God was condemned to work alone, *we* are not. The history
we'll make, will make us in return. Chaos
and Creation are now in our hands.

A Tale of Enchantment

There was rain, that was all.
Rain that didn't let up even when our homes, our streets and our
cities
had been swept out of reach.

We've learned to sleep to the sound of its drumming us through our
dreams,
to wake to its trickling away the seconds and minutes.
Days run through our fingers.
Night holds us fast.

The flooded graveyards give up their dead;
our children make a new life among rubble and mud.

When the rain stops, this tale of enchantment will end.
Stripped of flesh and spirit from that moment on,
we'll be the battleground between the old gods and the new.
We'll be the wounds they hack into each other,

and where the healing must begin.

Abandoned Property

I met him a moment ago, stumbling
his way down. A bad night by the look of things:
he hadn't slept, or else he hadn't woken
and the dreams had just kept coming.

Should I have stopped to say hello? Caught his eye?
Polite but firm, should I have grabbed him? Told him
to get himself back up those stairs where he belonged?

He pretended he hadn't even seen me.
A little late for that, I thought.
We were almost level when. . .

. . . he tripped, lost his balance, sprawled forwards –

Was he trusting that I'd catch him? That invisible angels
with invisible wings would bear him off to safety?
He showed his celebrated mastery of circumstance:
his arms stretched welcome-wide (in crucifixion-mode perhaps,
or poised to swallow-dive).

And so we passed. Him ready for the next miracle,
me without a backward glance.

★

Upstairs, I've walked into an empty room.
Abandoned property, let's call it: the sky crumpled upon the floor,
kicked and trampled on; holes where stars have been ripped out;
midwinter darkness torn to shreds,
constellations scored across the night.

Such stillness. No sense of loss, no consolation. Merely nothing.

If I stand here long enough will I remember
what happens next? Already,
it seems I have been here forever.

The King and Queen of Winter

When the King and Queen walk side by side their breaths cloud,
their feet trample silence.
A waterfall has hardened into organ pipes,
their swollen stops jammed with the massed sound
of next year's spring.
The king pauses, listens, smiles, approves.

Around them – old men weighted down with days, weeks, months
piled upon their heads and shoulders. 'They need,'
observes the Queen, 'that touch of the sun
they'll never get, this side of the mountain.'
The living are in attendance, merely;
the dead are cut and stacked.

A picnic of chocolate and cognac – the pleasures of a lawless reign.
The bridge they should return by thaws too soon.
When the King and Queen lie side by side they cling
together: their courtship a maddened dance
to a maddened tune . . .

The sun, in exile, burns into their dreams.

Our Week in the Swiss Mountains

When stars fall at our feet I take them home,
and thread them to the ceiling.

We cross a stream: it breaks off, follows us back
to flow along one wall, sun-polished and clear.

Snowstorms scour the corridor.
Our breath's the dark green scent of fir-trees.

★

On our last morning the mountain opposite, rising
from behind your shoulder, resists a final invitation
to join us for breakfast. There's no time left:
Opening the window I reach for what was never there,
grasping what will never be.

We are, it seems, the memories you and I alone can share:
that threat beneath the rotted wooden bridge we had to crawl across;
the blizzard-white path we didn't know we'd lost;
and water slowed down to a standstill, sealing the village
and ourselves in its transparency . . .

A week passed in the mountains.
We close the door behind us, lock it. We leave,
and we remain.

The Story of Our Street

The girl's left hand keeps her coat shut, the other's
empty. She's standing in the middle of the street,
the traffic breaking to a stop around her.
Hardly sixteen: bleached hair, bleached skin, fear.

The man she's with: badly healing cuts and anger
clenched into a face, pressed-in bruises
where the eyes should be.
She's telling him she's sorry, and being sworn at.

Nearby, a parliament of two men and a woman sits arguing
upon the pavement; they shout at her to grow up,
can't she? A taxi horn blares –
she doesn't move.

I drop my 50p into the parliamentary cup, and walk past.
Behind me, the street shuts like a book, the place marked
just at the point where he hits her
in the mouth.

When I'm back this evening, the story will have moved on:
there will be no girl, no man and no parliament
                              – only you and I
and everyone else, and the street around us growing darker
as the sun abandons it.

Five Years Later

I kneel down in the room my mother's died in,
not to pray, not to weep:
I touch her hand again and say her name aloud.

★

Five years later I'm catching up on Sarajevo,
current famines, weapon stockpiles (outside
the city's wounds are opening again:

hospitals and schools stand gutted;
addicts sweat, get sick; the mad
and destitute seek us out)

when all at once the paper I've been reading,
the kitchen I am sitting in, our tenement, our street
and Edinburgh itself seem set around me
as the walls of her room.

Too late to kneel down, too late to pray
to weep, to take her hand –

The loss I'm grieving for is still to come:

Sometimes I see it in another's eyes.
Sometimes I see it in my own.

Interrogation Outside the Mad Woman's House

She'd come running out the gate towards me;
she tried to ask me who I was
and where I came from. She'd been bending down
to touch me on the cheek
when someone rushed up, grabbed her
and forced her back indoors.

She died years later, at the same age she ever was. Today,
this cold rain blowing into my face
and these branches cutting the wind into her voice,
continue the interrogation.

Before the Programme Starts

When I hear articulate men discuss the kinds of war,
the kinds of peace worth settling for,
deciding among themselves what countries have to starve,
and who goes blind, gets poisoned, tortured, raped

– it's like listening to the adverts. Just that. And I know
they can't go on forever.
                              So,
before the actual programme starts,
before our lives have been explained
away, let's you and I agree upon what's left
for us to say:
No heartfelt declarations, please.
                              Come close,
there are no words for what matters most.

From What I Saw Today

He's curled at the edges, broken-spined and ready
to be withdrawn from circulation;
few have glanced beyond the early chapters;
the end will come as a surprise
to no-one. He's on loan, as it were,
to a public who've stopped reading books
like him. Date-stamped all those years ago, then carelessly
corrected, smudged and scribbled over -
the clear print's blurred to tiredness,
hesitation, an apology.

From what I saw today the pages are slipping out of sequence;
the story's making less and less sense.
Who can gather up the leaves, put them
in a sort of order?

There is no other copy to refer to.

The Circle Dante Wasn't Shown

Having reached this stretch of unrecorded ground,
this level stillness of relentless day, we've found
we are alone. Those raising up their hands are branded
by the sun, those falling on their knees in prayer
are kept there. The rest trudge forwards - heat
and searing light force us on . . .

Meanwhile: You're waiting for the phone to ring,
waiting for a letter, email, fax, any bloody thing
hinting at reprieve. Each day's a stay of execution:
the stop-and-go of traffic at the lights, the green man, red,
The Art of Fugue, The X Files, what the checkout woman said
about the bonus points redemption scheme. . .
You still believe no-one's to blame?
When *your* turn comes / your card gets swiped / you sign your name.

We are the circle Dante wasn't shown:
the understudies for no known part in no known play
- we're waiting to come on
and never will.

Meanwhile: Unpack the Tesco bag-for-life.
Unwrap the pre-cooked chicken, the 'no fuss'
prewashed, farmfresh mussels-in-their-shell.
Time to heat up, eat up and discuss
the world's affairs, and then your own.

Nearby, in hell, another evening falters to a standstill.

Meanwhile: Fade out the city streets, the sky, the background music of
the spheres. . .

We'll wait with you till everything around you disappears:
wait upon this stretch of unrecorded -
this level stillness of -
this heat and
searing
light

Our Piece of Good Fortune

Those of us who have learned to live without drawing breath—

Who start each day falling headlong towards certain destruction—

Who darken the clear morning skies like heavier rain—

We've come to grief so often we expect the concrete-slabbed
                                        pavements
to flatten us and the streets to run us down,
the empty stretches of the public parks to tidy us from sight,
and the soil of freshly dug gardens to bury us.
But no.

By lunchtime we're out and about, accosting friends and strangers,
telling them how lucky they are,
and how lucky we are.
We're wanting to share our piece of good fortune - and, after all
                                        these years,
are still surprised when the likes of him, the likes of her
and the likes of them all turn away.

Late afternoon is the worst.
At this low-point of the day we try touching base:
What's been achieved? we ask
looking around us.
And it's too early yet for that first drink of the evening. . .

Soon we're longing for a kindred spirit.
We're incandescent, you might say.
See us lighting up the night sky - a meteor shower, falling stars
for others to wish upon. So, go ahead. Why not make a wish?
- it seems we've little else to give you.

Those of us who've learned to get through the night do our best
to avoid draughts and awkward furniture in the dark.
When we settle down to sleep we hug our piece of good fortune
to us, as close as we can.

Three Composers Respond to the Politics of Perpetual War

1. How Schoenberg's Twelve-Note Series Might Have Led to a Better World, but Didn't

Arnold Schoenberg, like everyone else at the end of the nineteenth
century,
had taken his seat on the crowded train heading towards
an ever-better world. As it turned the corner into the glorious future
ahead,
the engine started picking up speed – moments later slamming
into a solid wall.

Bits went everywhere: bits of countries, bits of colonies, bits of
science, art and religion. The tracks, seeming to stretch back to the
beginnings of Time,
were wrenched apart; buckled and bent,
they clawed at the blue sky above Passchendaele.

Suddenly the street was full of people who knew best. Their self-
appointed task: to get civilisation back on the rails. They all agreed
that drastic problems need drastic solutions – and each had a solution
more drastic than the one before.

Such a noise of hammering and welding! Such a clamour and din of
revolution, extermination, colonial expansion and unemployment; of
mass production and racial purity! The Stock Exchange boomed, the
trains ran on time.

Schoenberg, meanwhile, was discarding tonality. He declared that his
twelve-note system would create a melodic line strong enough to
hold everything together. Even Chaos itself.

Around him, the street was bustling with strikers and strike-breakers,
cattle trucks criss-crossing Europe, financiers thudding onto
pavements, parades, searchlights, flags, roaring ovens, transatlantic
crossings to the sounds of the restaurant orchestra, reasoned debate
and orderly soup queues.

Soon Schoenberg was rushing up to complete strangers: 'My twelve-
note system offers real value for money to composer, player and
audience alike.'

Darkness fell swifter than ever before. Once the lights went out, The Sandman tiptoed from country to country tucking the sleepers tight in their beds. That done, he began telling them their dreams.

Schoenberg closed his eyes believing the time would come when mothers crooned his twelve-note lullabies to their children. This particular dream made even The Sandman smile.

2. Between Hollywood Immortality and Life and Death on Wall Street – The Early Days of John Cage

The third day in Cage's life began before
the second had finished. Counterpoint of a sort,
he remarked to himself while watching a half-completed dream
get spiked onto the city skyline.

For the next week his nursery was ransacked
by the impatient future. Teddy's glass eye winked
at shutter-speed: record-erase / record-erase /
record-erase . . . Deformed as we all are
by our longings, Cage wept childish tears
for the rest of his life. As we all do.

He knew, when aged a fortnight, that he already knew too much:
– The city skyline, that bundle of I-Ching sticks, was ready to be
thrown;
– America, that bloodred carpet laid down to welcome the 20th
century,
fitted perfectly (it was the world, of course, that needed trimmed).
The future was always a step ahead:
a part-developed print, a ghost
that left tracks.

Let's pretend, he said to himself while clutching
the bars that kept him safer than love,
let's pretend the West Coast and the East (Hollywood immortality,
life and death on Wall St) are lines drawn in the desert: traced out
and erased /
traced out and erased / traced out and erased . . .

The sands of Time, the arithmetic of Chance.

The Desert of New Mexico:
The Manhattan Project + Los Alamos = Hiroshima
The Desert of Nevada:
Las Vegas + this (for-one-lifetime-only) 4-dimensional dice
 = our aging towards a certainty.

Meanwhile from the sand grain's empty heart, from its lifeless core
— Silence / Silence / Silence

3. Stockhausen's Soundtrack for the Post-Apocalypse Will Be Written in Strict Symphonic Form

Opening Allegro perpetuo

Cut and loop the TV clips to send that second plane
into that second tower inside our head. Now every plane
in every empty sky, flowers red
and yellow flames inside our head.

And so -

Cut and loop the TV clips etc. etc. etc. . .

Adagio

Five billion dollars' darkness glides five miles above:
no stain across the radar sky, no sonic boom disturbing us
five miles below. No unnecessary din.
We're free to look on while our town, our street, our work-place,
and our homes are re-designed with state-of-the-art efficiency:
our grandparents, our children, husbands, wives, friends, arms, legs,
                                                  eyes, hands, skin.

Scherzo and Trio

Switch off the moon, turn up the sun,
Stockhausen's soundtrack has begun.

New York and Kabul are suburbs of the same city.
Cluster bombs and food parcels drop
from the same planes.

Cancel the earth, delete the stars,
Stockhausen's soundtrack will do for all wars.

Closing allegro

That clear September morning in Manhattan.
The night-sky above the Afghan desert, above Baghdad.
We turn from one to see the other. There's nothing else.
Stockhausen's soundtrack. End-of-tape hiss . . . .

Contemporary Music in Scotland

In the absence of an orchestra in his muddy Scottish village
the boy conducts the trees, his string section.
Gradually the cattle on the hillside, the birds, the wind, the river,
the farmer's dog, the sound of rain - everything seen and unseen
is given its place on his unwritten score.

At school he has the finger pointed at him. The teacher,
a believer in Scottish Education, stands him out in front
to conduct the morning's noise. He'll be kept there till he's learned
his lesson: enough tears, and a sneer will pass for kindness
and red hair turn to flame.

Houses are made from the ruins of other houses,
from the rubble and brickwork of the castle.
The mad are penned together near the flooded field;
the others buy and sell daylight, trading colour
for colour. Dusk alone brings close of business.

The fire burns low. He stares into a darkness silvered here and there
by stars and transatlantic flight paths. He cannot sleep for listening
to the restless hills and streams, to their unplayed music,
to the moon far above and turning
soundlessly on its invisible rope.

The Voice Inside

1. *Largo*

Hush . . . Hush . . .
Hush the strings . . .
Hush the body . . .
Still the bow to silence echoing
the silence long before
the strings, the body and the bow.
Before the strings were laid in place,
pegged and tied,
stretched and tightened taut.
Before arching them into the emptiness all around,
holding the greater silence
echoing the greatest silence
ever.

Then touch – Hush – Touch – Hush
Touch . . . Stroke to sound . . . Draw sound out of
tightness, out of stillness, out of emptiness . . .
Shaping the emptiness that everything
comes from and returns to. Giving it scale,
giving voice. Giving life.

2. *Scherzo I: Duet*

Your voice / My voice
Sound plaited with sound
Silence layered upon silence
criss-crossing, parting,
sliding together
to harmonise,
to kiss.

And O, those fugal lines
of tig and catch,
touch and snatch,
tag and miss.

Catch as catch can,
boy and girl, woman, man.

Your theme or mine?

Line for line into the bars
and out.

Your key or mine?
– let's intertwine!

3. *Vigorous*

Not a woman's voice – no:
Hard and harshness
Stride and strident.

Not a woman's voice – no:
Slash, strike, cut, score.

Not pleading, not pleasing, not –

Wound to the heart.
Stab to the soul.

Scar, scrape, mark, march
Destroy, destroy, destroy.

4. *Slow Movement*

All sound has always held itself as absence:
in the slackened strings, in hollowed body,
in unstrung bow. And as presence:
soul as silence.

5. *Scherzo II*

Four strings, body and bow.
Locatelli, Corelli,
Paganini, Tartini,
Neil Gow, Neil Gow, Neil Gow.

Four strings, body and bow.
Guarneri, Amati,
Stradivari, Viotti,
Vivaldi, Grapelli,
Spohr, Spivakovsky,
Neil Gow, Neil Gow, Neil Gow.

6. *BURLESQUE*

Twelve equal tones dangling on a score,
if one of them should modulate
- would there be a melody
where none had been before?

Twelve equal tones dangling on a stave,
if all of them should modulate
 - which one would we save?

Chaos comes but once a year,
Creation's always late
so choose the note you like to hear
 - the rest will sublimate!

7. *PLEA*

Hear my voice, hear me listening
to the voice inside,
so deep, deep inside:

Rising up from the core of the earth it feels,
from the furthest rim of the farthest star it feels,
from the darkest hour, the darkest night

the radiant sun at noon
- into my heart, into my lungs, my throat

Revealing what I do not know.
Expressing what I dare not feel.
Saying what cannot keep silent.

Cassandra's Lament

What I see is what I say –
Five continents of sense becoming one.
My own, this sixth sense – mine alone.
Shadows without sun, their every touch contagion –
some chill, some burn. Only the scars are mine:
invisible as loss – or hope.

Cassandra's Gifts

The King – A crown of iron and splintered bone.
The Queen – A robe of spattered blood.
My gifts for my royal masters.
To curse them. To call them to their time.
The rest, the undisclosed, is mine:
Slavery, exile and the blessings of the unseen.

Heroes of the West: High Noon to Midnight

High Noon: The tall dark stranger's come to save the town.
Wind him up and watch him strut
his stuff on Main St!

Close-focus on the eyes, the hands, the gun . . . Hit leather!
Crack! One badman's down,
the next, a third. It's done. Give the man a badge!
(Democracy's too precious to be left to chance.)

Fast forward to the 24-hour war on cable.
The hero's come to save the world
with miracles:
> \- Any Main St in any town . . .
> \- Any Royal Palace (that's where the badmen hide in fear,
> their toes curling up their oriental slippers) . . .
He'll make these badlands disappear (more magic in one split-second
than in a thousand and one nights).

High Noon (that's when the world was black and white)
has ticked its way to midnight. Now darkness makes the best TV:
the blinded, the mutilated and the maimed are safely
out of sight. The seagreen techno-light that's best for shooting,
is best for killing . . .

. . . But here's our hero, he strides in to command
the microphones, to speak the good speak:
'We have the technology, and we have God.
Make no mistake - we mean business.
Make no mistake - Democracy's for Oil! (for *All*,
he meant to say, of course). We thank you.'

He leaves us. He walks the good walk. He walks alone
- a bantam-strut that's all his very own.

A Child's Song: What No One Can Know

Look in the mirror, breathe on the glass,
there you will see what must come to pass.
Are you a smile, a laugh or a frown?
Will you grow up or will you grow down?

At night when you sleep, the world is your own:
no sunlight or moonlight – *your* light alone.
What do you see when you close your eyes?
– for this is a darkness that cannot tell lies.

Where have you come from? Where will you go?
These are unknowns that no one can know.
But sometimes a moment will come when it seems
you *know* who you are, and the rest is all dreams.

And when it does, then don't turn away,
don't be afraid to stand up and say:
'I am who I am, and know I am free
to be who I will – and I will be ME!'

Index of Titles